UNDEFEATED!

How to Win Every Battle and Never Back Down

GBENGA SHOWUNMI

UNDEFEATED!

Published by Cornerstone Publishing

A Division of Cornerstone Creativity Group LLC
Info@thecornerstonepublishers.com
www.thecornerstonepublishers.com

Author's Contact

To book the author to speak at your next event or to order bulk copies of this book, please, use the information below:

pastorshow@gmail.com | gbengashowunmi.com

Printed in the United States of America.

For whatever is born of God overcomes the world. And this is the victory that has overcome the world—our faith.

—1 John 5:4

CONTENTS

INTRODUCTION vii

1. BORN TO WIN.. 1

2. THE BATTLE IS THE LORD'S........................13

3. FEARLESS FAITH 23

4. SET THE LORD BEFORE YOU 39

5. SPEAK LIFE, LIVE POWERFULLY..............51

6. THE WINNING MINDSET..............................65

7. NEVER ALONE, ALWAYS BACKED............77

8. VICTORY IN SPIRITUAL WARFARE............87

9. UNDEFEATED AND UNSTOPPABLE........99

CONCLUSION 111

INTRODUCTION

IF GOD BE FOR US...

"What shall we then say to these things? If God be for us, who can be against us?"

— ROMANS 8:31, KJV

Life is not just a gentle stroll in the park; it's more like a battlefield where destinies are fought for, identities are challenged, and faith is tested. Yet, for the child of God, there's a covenant promise: you are not alone in this fight. You are not unarmed. You are not at a disadvantage. If God is on your side, nothing and no one can ultimately stand against you.

This book was forged in the fires of experience. It resonates with the heartbeat of those who have endured pain yet never lost their praise. It speaks to every believer who refuses to give in to fear, failure, or spiritual intimidation. You are called to rise, not retreat. You are called to reign, not run. You are called to win, not waver.

The Word of God declares:

"For whatsoever is born of God overcometh the world: and this is the victory that overcometh the world, even our faith"
— *(1 John 5:4).*

Your victory does not depend on your circumstances, your connections, or your own strength. It is rooted in Christ, secured by the cross, sealed by His blood, and sustained by the Spirit.

Consider David standing before Goliath. The odds were stacked against him, yet he triumphed because the anointing was with him.

Think of Esther before the king. Her past did not hinder her courage; she was on a divine mission.

Daniel survived the lion's den, not because the lions were tame, but because God shut their mouths.

Paul and Silas sang their way out of prison, and the earth responded to their praise.

These are not fairy tales; they are divine patterns that reveal the nature of our God, who transforms underdogs into champions, victims into victors, and worshipers into warriors.

If you're weary from battles, discouraged by delays, or tempted to give up, this book is for you. It is a call to stand firm in the authority God has given you. It is a guide for spiritual warriors ready to walk in dominion. It is a prophetic reminder of who you are and whose you are.

"I have set the Lord always before me: because he is at my right hand, I shall not be moved."

— Psalm 16:8

You are not abandoned. You are supported by heaven.

You are not defeated. You are destined for victory.

You are not a statistic. You are a sign and a wonder.

You are not weak. You are strong in the Lord and in the power of His might.

This is your moment. Step into it with faith. Read with expectancy. Engage with boldness.

Heaven is cheering you on. The Spirit of God is within you.

You are about to discover what it truly means to live...

UNDEFEATED!

CHAPTER ONE

BORN TO WIN

"Nay, in all these things we are more than conquerors through him that loved us."
— ROMANS 8:37 (KJV)

In 1934, a young African-American boy named Jesse Owens stood at the starting line of the Big Ten Championships, battling a sore back and the weight of racial discrimination. Victory felt distant, almost unattainable. Yet, in just 45 minutes, he achieved the extraordinary, breaking three world records and tying a fourth. This moment is still celebrated as "the greatest 45 minutes ever in sport."

What fueled his determination? Owens later reflected, *"The battles that count aren't the ones for gold medals. The struggles within yourself—the invisible, inevitable battles inside all of us; that's where it's won."*

You don't need perfect conditions to succeed. What matters is knowing deep down that you were meant for greatness. That's where true victory begins, not in your surroundings, but in your sense of self.

You were never meant to live as a defeated Christian. You were born again into a kingdom of power, called to dominate, and raised up to win. Winning is not just what you do—it is who you are in Christ. The moment you gave your life to Jesus, a divine transformation took place. Your old self died, and a new, victorious self came alive. You are not trying to become a winner; you were born into victory.

The Bible states in 2 Corinthians 5:17, *"Therefore if any man be in Christ, he is a new creature: old things are passed away; behold, all things are become new."* This new creation reality is not merely a religious concept; it is a supernatural transformation. Your spiritual DNA has changed. You carry the life of God within you, and that life is victorious. It cannot be overcome by darkness.

YOU WERE NEVER DESIGNED FOR DEFEAT

God never intended for His children to live under the burden of fear, shame, or oppression. When He created man, He gave him dominion.

"And God said, Let us make man in our image, after our likeness: and let them have dominion..." — *Genesis 1:26*

You were made to rule, not to be ruled by life's circumstances. Sin corrupted that design, but Jesus came to restore it. At the cross, Jesus did not just save you from sin; He empowered you to live a victorious life.

This is why Colossians 2:15 tells us, *"And having spoiled principalities and powers, he made a shew of them openly, triumphing over them in it."* Jesus didn't win quietly; He made a public spectacle of Satan's defeat. That victory is yours. You are seated with Christ in heavenly places (Ephesians 2:6), far above all principalities and powers.

So why do many believers still live beneath their rights?

Because the enemy knows that if you ever fully grasp your identity, his days of dominance are over.

DAVID: A YOUNG MAN WITH A WINNER'S SPIRIT

One of the clearest examples of the "born to win" mindset is David. He was the least likely candidate, the forgotten son, the one not even invited to the anointing ceremony. Yet God chose him and anointed him. When the time came, David didn't shy away from battle.

When Goliath mocked Israel, David didn't see a giant—he saw an opportunity for God's power to be revealed. He declared, *"Thy servant slew both the lion and the bear… the Lord that delivered me… will deliver me out of the hand of this Philistine"* (1 Samuel 17:36–37).

That's the language of someone who knows they were born to win.

David didn't wait until he was on the throne to believe he was a king. He lived like a victor long before he wore the crown. That's what it means to have a covenant mindset. You don't speak based on your bank account, your background, or your current battle. You speak from your position in Christ.

VICTORY IS YOUR SPIRITUAL INHERITANCE

Romans 5:17 says, *"…they which receive abundance of grace and of the gift of righteousness shall reign in life by one, Jesus Christ."* To reign in life means to rule, to walk in dominion, to live above oppression, to overcome opposition, and to fulfill your destiny.

This reign is not just for pastors, prophets, or church

leaders. It belongs to every believer who has received the abundance of grace and the gift of righteousness. If you are in Christ, this is your inheritance.

You were not born again to struggle endlessly with sin, to be trapped in cycles of defeat, or to accept the lies of the enemy. You were born again to reign. To conquer. To win.

JESUS: THE UNDEFEATED CHAMPION

Our ultimate example is Jesus Christ. He walked the earth with divine authority, never intimidated by demons, never afraid of opposition. The winds obeyed Him. Sickness fled at His command. The dead heard His voice and lived. And even when the enemy thought he had cornered Him at the cross, Jesus rose from the grave in power.

Hebrews 2:14 tells us, *"…that through death he might destroy him that had the power of death, that is, the devil."*

At the resurrection, Jesus didn't just come back to life; He returned as the undefeated Champion of heaven and earth. And when you said yes to Jesus, His victory became your victory. You now share in His triumph.

This is not just motivational talk; it is a scriptural truth.

"As he is, so are we in this world."

— *1 John 4:17*

If Jesus is not defeated, then you should not live defeated. If Jesus is not beneath circumstances, then neither are you.

WHY BELIEVERS SOMETIMES LIVE DEFEATED

Many believers struggle not because they lack power, but because they lack understanding. The enemy thrives on ignorance. That is why Paul prayed in Ephesians 1:17–18, *"That the God of our Lord Jesus Christ… may give unto you the spirit of wisdom and revelation… that ye may know…"*

The devil knows he cannot steal your victory, but he will try to hide it from you. He does this by sowing lies:

"You'll never overcome this addiction."

"You're too damaged to be used by God."

"Your background disqualifies you."

But truth silences every lie. You are accepted in the Beloved (Ephesians 1:6). You are complete in Christ (Colossians 2:10). You are more than a conqueror

(Romans 8:37). You are the head and not the tail (Deuteronomy 28:13). You are blessed with all spiritual blessings in heavenly places (Ephesians 1:3).

The more you renew your mind with the Word, the more your inner self will rise in boldness. Faith is not a feeling; it is confidence in what God has said. And faith comes by hearing, and hearing by the Word of God (Romans 10:17).

FROM VICTIM TO VICTOR

The Bible is filled with stories of people who seemed defeated but ultimately rose in triumph.

Joseph was sold into slavery, falsely accused, and thrown into prison. Yet, he rose to become prime minister in Egypt. Why? Because the Lord was with him. His setbacks became setups for God's greater plan.

Gideon was hiding from the enemy when God called him a mighty man of valor. As he believed the Word of the Lord, he rose from fear into leadership and led a small army to an impossible victory.

Ruth was a widow in a foreign land, but she clung to her covenant. Her faith positioned her for redemption, marriage, and motherhood in the lineage of the Messiah.

These are not isolated stories. They are testimonies of what happens when the hand of God rests on someone who refuses to quit. The difference between being crushed and being crowned is often found in your response to adversity.

HOW TO WALK IN VICTORY DAILY

Winning in the Spirit is not automatic. It does not happen by accident, emotion, or wishful thinking. Victory must be enforced. Although Jesus has already won the battle, it is your responsibility as a believer to walk in that victory every day. The enemy thrives on passivity, but he cannot prevail against a Christian who is spiritually alert, rooted in truth, and armed with faith. Here are three essential keys that will help you walk in consistent spiritual victory.

KNOW YOUR IDENTITY

Everything starts with identity. If the enemy can confuse who you are, he can manipulate how you live. That is why your first weapon is **revelation**—knowing who you are in Christ. You are not your past. You are not your failures. You are not what others say about you. You are a new creation, born of the Spirit, redeemed by the blood, and destined for greatness. You are a child of God, filled with resurrection power, clothed in righteousness, and seated with Christ in heavenly places. When you truly know your identity, you stop tolerating bondage and start walking in authority. You no longer live from a place of defeat but from your position of victory.

SPEAK THE WORD

The Word of God is not just information—it is a weapon. Jesus did not defeat Satan in the wilderness with emotion or human reasoning. He said, *"It is written."* That simple but powerful phrase broke the back of temptation and exposed the devil's lies. In the same way, the Word in your mouth carries divine authority when spoken in faith. When you declare what God has said, you align your life with heaven's truth and release spiritual power into your circumstances. Do not let your voice echo your fears; let it declare God's promises. Speak the Word over your mind, your body, your finances, your family, and your future. Victory is voice-activated.

STAY IN THE PRESENCE

Intimacy fuels authority. Your ability to stand firm in the day of battle is directly connected to your consistency in the secret place. Psalm 91 reminds us that those who dwell in the secret place of the Most High shall abide under the shadow of the Almighty. To dwell means to live there, not to visit occasionally. It means setting your heart on God, seeking Him daily, and cultivating an unbroken connection with His presence. The devil is not afraid of church attendance alone, but he trembles before a believer who abides in God. In His presence, you receive strength, clarity, joy, direction, and divine support. You do not just fight from the battlefield—you fight from the throne room.

FAITH DECLARATION

Say this out loud:

- I am born of God.

- I am not trying to win—I have already won in Christ.

- I am more than a conqueror.

- The Spirit of God lives in me.

- I am strong, fearless, and favored.

- I am destined to reign.

- I live undefeated in Jesus' name.

PRAYER POINTS:
BORN TO WIN

1. Father, I thank You because I am not a mistake—I was born with a purpose, and I declare that I will fulfill it in Jesus' name.

2. Every lie from the enemy trying to convince me that I'm not enough—I silence it now with the truth of God's Word. I am born to win!

3. I receive fresh revelation of my identity in Christ. I am part of a royal priesthood, a chosen generation, and more than a conqueror!

4. Lord, awaken the champion within me. Let the fire of divine confidence consume every fear, doubt, and limitation.

5. I declare that my past failures will not define my future victories. I shake off every garment of shame and rise in boldness!

6. By the power of the Holy Spirit, I step into my God-given assignment. I will not delay. I will not retreat. I will not be denied.

7. Father, align my thoughts with Your truth. Let my mindset reflect my identity as a winner, not a victim.

8. Every generational curse, label, or limitation placed on my life—I break it now by the authority in the name of Jesus!

9. I decree that I will walk in victory daily. I will run and not grow weary. I will rise and not faint.

10. Lord, let the testimony of my life reflect Your glory. Make me living proof that an undefeated life is possible through faith in You!

CHAPTER TWO

THE BATTLE IS
THE LORD'S

"Be not afraid nor dismayed by reason of this great multitude; for the battle is not yours, but God's."

— 2 CHRONICLES 20:15 (KJV)

In 1863, amid the harsh realities of the American Civil War, a Union soldier posed a poignant question to President Abraham Lincoln: Did he believe God was on their side? Lincoln took a moment *to reflect before responding, "Sir, my concern is not whether God is on our side; my greatest concern is to be on God's side, for God is always right."*

The course of that war shifted—not merely due to greater numbers, but through a sense of divine guidance and purpose. Lincoln understood something that many overlook: true victory doesn't come solely from strength or skill; it comes from surrendering to God's will.

When we relinquish control and trust the battle to the Lord, we invite the Commander of Heaven's armies to lead the way. And when God is in the fight, defeat becomes an impossibility.

Every believer reaches a moment when they must choose: will you fight your battles in your own strength, or will you surrender them to God? True victory is found not in striving, but in surrender. The battles that matter are those we yield to the Commander of Heaven's armies.

Jehoshaphat, the king of Judah, found himself surrounded by a vast army of enemies—the Moabites, Ammonites, and others. Outnumbered and ill-prepared for battle, he turned to the only true source of deliverance: God. The Word of the Lord came to him, saying, "You shall not need to fight in this battle: set yourselves, stand ye still, and see the salvation of the Lord with you" (2 Chronicles 20:17).

When God takes charge, defeat becomes impossible.

TRUSTING GOD WHEN YOU FEEL OUTNUMBERED

You don't have to look far to find a struggle. Every believer encounters opposition. Sometimes it comes from people; other times, it's internal—fear, anxiety, temptation, doubt. There are also demonic forces that create storms, delay breakthroughs, and target your faith. But none of these forces is stronger than the God who fights for you.

"If God be for us, who can be against us?"
— Romans 8:31

The truth is, life presents challenges that are too big for your human capacity. This is by divine design. God allows battles you cannot win on your own to teach you to trust Him completely.

Gideon faced an army of 135,000 Midianites with only 300 men. But God said, "The people that are with thee are too many… lest Israel vaunt themselves against me" (Judges 7:2). God intentionally reduced Gideon's resources so that the victory would point to Him.

You may feel outnumbered right now. But numbers don't sway God. He's never needed a crowd to win. All He requires is your faith.

GOD FIGHTS THROUGH YOUR OBEDIENCE

Often, God doesn't fight for us in the way we expect. He works through our obedience. When Israel marched around the walls of Jericho for seven days, it seemed foolish to the natural mind. But their obedience released divine strategy, and the walls fell flat (Joshua 6:20).

Victory is often hidden behind instruction. God may not require you to swing a sword, but He may ask you to fast, forgive, sow a seed, let go of a grudge, or lift your hands in praise when it hurts the most.

Obedience is not weakness; it is warfare. Every time you obey the voice of God, you align yourself with His supernatural plan.

SPIRITUAL WARFARE IS WON IN THE SPIRIT

You are not just a physical being; you are spirit, soul, and body. Your real battles are spiritual in nature.

"For we wrestle not against flesh and blood, but against principalities, against powers, against the rulers of the darkness of this world, against spiritual wickedness in high places." — Ephesians 6:12

This means your victories must also be spiritual. You don't conquer fear with arguments; you overcome it with truth. You don't break demonic oppression with anger; you dismantle it with the Word of God and the authority of Jesus' name.

David did not kill Goliath through swordplay. He defeated him first with faith-filled words. "Thou comest to me with a sword... but I come to thee in the name of the Lord of hosts" (1 Samuel 17:45). The battle was won in the spirit before it was ever seen in the natural.

You cannot fight spiritual battles with carnal weapons. You must engage with spiritual tools—prayer, fasting, worship, declarations, the Word of God, and the blood of Jesus.

YOUR JOB: STAND, BELIEVE, AND DECLARE

Sometimes, the toughest part of the battle is not the fighting; it's the waiting. Trusting. Standing firm in faith when nothing seems to change. But victory belongs to those who stand their ground.

Ephesians 6:13 says, "...having done all, to stand."

You might not feel strong, but your faith is. You may not see results yet, but heaven is at work. The angels are active. The Spirit is speaking.

God hasn't asked you to figure everything out. He has asked you to believe. You are not the general in this battle; God is. Your role is to stay aligned, keep your praise high, speak in agreement with His Word, and refuse to give in to fear.

Isaiah 41:10 is your promise: "Fear not; for I am with you: be not dismayed; for I am your God: I will strengthen you... I will uphold you with the right hand of my righteousness."

LET GOD BE GOD

Sometimes, we find ourselves in battles that aren't meant for us. We try to control, fix, argue, or manipulate. But God's Word says, "Vengeance is mine; I will repay" (Romans 12:19). There are fights you don't need to engage in. Let God be God. He is more skilled in delivering justice. He is wiser in judgment. He sees the end from the beginning.

In 2 Chronicles 20, Jehoshaphat placed singers ahead of the army. While that may seem illogical in a military context, it makes perfect sense in God's kingdom. When we praise, God acts. When we worship, He moves. When we trust, He prevails.

FAITH DECLARATION

- The battle is not mine; it belongs to the Lord.

- I will not fear the arrows of the enemy.

- I will not be swayed by what I see.

- God is fighting for me.

- I stand in victory.

- I am protected, provided for, and preserved.

- No weapon formed against me shall prosper.

- I am undefeated because the Lord of hosts is on my side.

PRAYER POINTS:
THE BATTLE IS THE LORD'S

1. Father, I thank You because no battle in my life is too great for You to win.

2. Lord, I surrender every visible and invisible battle to You. Fight for me and grant me peace.

3. I silence every voice of fear and intimidation with the authority of Your Word.

4. Father, send forth Your angelic forces to fight on my behalf and thwart the enemy's plans.

5. I declare that every siege around my life, family, and destiny breaks by fire in Jesus' name.

6. I receive divine strategies to walk in obedience and victory, just like Jehoshaphat and David.

7. Every Goliath standing against my breakthrough, fall by the power in the name of Jesus.

8. Lord, fill my mouth with praise and teach my hands to engage in worship.

9. By the blood of Jesus, I cancel every evil verdict and demonic opposition over my life.

10. I boldly declare: I am undefeated because the battle is the Lord's. Hallelujah!

CHAPTER THREE

FEARLESS FAITH

"For God hath not given us the spirit of fear; but of power, and of love, and of a sound mind."

— 2 TIMOTHY 1:7 (KJV)

In 1950, a young missionary named Jim Elliot left the comfort of America to reach an unreached tribe deep in the Ecuadorian jungle. People called it foolish, and the tribe was known to be violent. But Jim was driven by one conviction: *"He is no fool who gives what he cannot keep to gain what he cannot lose."*

Jim and four others were eventually killed by the very people they tried to reach. But that wasn't the end. Years later, their families returned and led the entire tribe to Christ. The seed of fearless faith bore eternal fruit.

Fearless faith doesn't always look like winning in the moment. Sometimes it seems like risking everything with your eyes on eternity. But it always shakes hell and advances the Kingdom.

Fear is one of Satan's most effective weapons. It paralyzes faith, magnifies the enemy, and silences our destiny. Yet, every believer is called to live boldly—not by our own strength, but by a supernatural confidence in God's Word. Fearless faith does not mean a lack of challenges; rather, it is the refusal to let fear dictate the outcome.

When you truly understand who God is and who you are in Him, fear loses its grip. The righteous are as bold as lions (Proverbs 28:1). You were not reborn to be timid, anxious, or afraid. You were recreated in Christ to stand confidently, operate in power, and walk in dominion—even when facing opposition.

FAITH AND FEAR CANNOT COEXIST

Fear and faith cannot share the same heart. One will always silence the other.

Faith says, *"God is with me."*

Fear says, *"What if I fail?"*

Faith says, *"All things are possible."*

Fear says, *"This might not work."*

Faith aligns with heaven. Fear aligns with hell.

Hebrews 11:6 declares, *"But without faith it is impossible to please him…"* God does not take a neutral stance on fear. Fear is not just an emotion; it is a spiritual force that must be resisted with the same determination as sin.

In Mark 4, when the disciples were terrified during the storm, Jesus rebuked the wind and then addressed their fear: *"Why are ye so fearful? how is it that ye have no faith?"* (Mark 4:40). He understood that fear and faith are opposites. Fear endures the storm; faith speaks to it.

BIBLICAL EXAMPLES OF FEARLESS FAITH

1. Daniel in the Lion's Den

Daniel was thrown into a den of lions because of his unwavering prayer life. Yet, he did not plead for his life or compromise his beliefs. He trusted God, and God shut the mouths of the lions. When faith speaks louder than fear, deliverance follows.

2. The Three Hebrew Boys

Shadrach, Meshach, and Abednego stood firm against the golden image of Nebuchadnezzar. They boldly declared, *"Our God whom we serve is able to deliver* us… *but if not, be it known… we will not serve thy gods"* (Daniel 3:17–18). This exemplifies fearless faith. Whether God intervenes immediately or not, they refused to back down. As a result, the Son of God appeared in the fire, and they emerged unscathed, without even a trace of smoke on them.

3. David Facing Goliath

While the trained soldiers of Israel cowered in fear, young David stepped forward with a slingshot and a declaration: *"The battle is the Lord's, and he will give you into our hands"* (1 Samuel 17:47). He didn't wait for victory to believe in it—he proclaimed it before it came to pass.

Faith always speaks before it sees.

FEARLESS FAITH SPEAKS, MOVES, AND STANDS

Fearless faith is active. It speaks with confidence, acts with courage, and remains steadfast.

1. It Speaks

Jesus taught in Mark 11:23, *"Whosoever shall say unto this mountain, Be thou removed… and shall not doubt… he shall have whatsoever he saith."* Faith expresses itself. It doesn't stay silent in the face of challenges.

2. It Moves

Faith without action is lifeless (James 2:17). Fearless faith takes steps even when the outcome is uncertain. Just like Peter stepping out of the boat, bold faith moves at the command of Christ.

3. It Stands

Ephesians 6:13 instructs us to *"stand therefore…"* Faith does not retreat when results are delayed. It does not falter when faced with resistance. It stands firmly on God's promises, trusting that His Word will not return void (Isaiah 55:11).

ENEMIES OF FEARLESS FAITH

To cultivate fearless faith, you must silence its adversaries:

1. Doubt

Doubt is the enemy's stealthy assassin. It doesn't always roar like fear; sometimes, it softly whispers, *"Did God really say?"* Just like in the Garden of Eden, Satan used doubt to divert destiny. He didn't wield a sword—he posed a question. Doubt works subtly, eroding faith bit by bit, causing believers to question what they once held with certainty. James 1:6–7 warns, *"But let him ask in faith, nothing wavering… For let not that man think that he shall receive any thing of the Lord."* Doubt is not only perilous—it disqualifies when allowed to linger.

Jesus often addressed the doubt in His disciples, especially after they had seen His miracles up close. When Peter walked on water and started to sink, Jesus asked, *"O thou of little faith, wherefore didst thou doubt?"* (Matthew 14:31). Peter's struggle didn't stem from the storm itself but from allowing what he saw to undermine what he believed. That's the nature of doubt; it questions the reliability of God's Word. To conquer doubt, you must nourish your faith and diminish your fears. Doubt cannot flourish in a heart filled with the Word.

2. Delay

Delay is not denial, but if we misinterpret it, it can feel like defeat. God isn't rushed, but He is always timely. The challenge is that we often anticipate immediate results, and when answers take longer than expected, fear can creep in. Sarah laughed at the idea of having a son because it seemed delayed beyond reason. Yet, Romans 4:20 tells us about Abraham, *"He staggered not at the promise of God through unbelief; but was strong in faith, giving glory to God."* His faith was strong even in the face of delay.

Faith doesn't crumble under the pressure of time.

True faith recognizes that every delay serves a divine purpose. Sometimes, God uses delay to cultivate endurance, deepen trust, or clear the path ahead. Waiting isn't wasting time when you're journeying with God. Isaiah 40:31 assures us, *"But they that wait upon the Lord shall renew their strength…"* Delay tests our confidence. Will you still trust when the promise seems far off? Fearless faith asserts, *"Though it tarries, I will wait for it, because it will surely come."* (see Habakkuk 2:3)

3. Sight

What you see can often be deceptive. Faith thrives in the unseen, while fear feeds off visible circumstances. 2 Corinthians 5:7 reminds us that *"we walk by faith, not by sight."* When Peter focused on Jesus, he walked on water. But when he turned his gaze to the waves, he began to sink. Sight can be a powerful influence, and if left unchecked, it can distort your spiritual understanding. Sight may say, "There's no money in the account." Faith counters, "My God shall supply all my need." Sight might declare, "The doctor's report is grim." Faith responds, "By His stripes I am healed."

This doesn't mean we deny facts; it means we embrace a deeper truth. The natural world is real, but it is always changing. Hebrews 11:3 tells us that the worlds were framed by the Word of God, indicating that what we see was made from what we cannot see. Your faith should be anchored in God's Word, not solely on what your senses perceive. Living by sight can limit God, while living by faith opens the door to the supernatural. Fearless faith chooses to believe even when the evidence isn't visible.

4. Human Opinion

One of the greatest pitfalls for any believer is the fear of man. Proverbs 29:25 states, *"The fear of man bringeth a snare: but whoso putteth his trust in the Lord shall be safe."* Many destinies have been delayed, diluted, or destroyed by the need to please others. When you place human opinion above God's guidance, you become trapped by the approval of others. Saul lost his kingdom because he feared the people and disobeyed God (1 Samuel 15:24). Faith cannot thrive in a heart that seeks to conform to the crowd.

Jesus was never swayed by the opinions of others. He healed on the Sabbath, reached out to outcasts, and challenged religious leaders—all because He aimed to please the Father. Fearless faith must be grounded in divine approval, not societal validation. Galatians 1:10 asks, *"Do I seek to please men? for if I yet pleased men, I should not be the servant of Christ."* Faith looks up, not around. It prioritizes obedience over popularity and purpose over acceptance. If you want to live a life of fearless faith, you must embrace this truth: God's opinion is the only one that truly counts.

DEVELOPING A FEARLESS FAITH LIFESTYLE

Fearless faith is not just a supernatural gift reserved for apostles and prophets. It is a spiritual discipline—a lifestyle that every believer can develop with intention, consistency, and revelation. God has not called you to live in fear, anxiety, or hesitation. He has called you to walk boldly, speak courageously, and advance in unstoppable power.

Here are five ways to cultivate a fearless faith lifestyle:

1. Meditate on the Word Daily

Joshua 1:8 declares, *"This book of the law shall not depart out of thy mouth; but thou shalt meditate therein day and night... then thou shalt make thy way prosperous, and then thou shalt have good success."* Fear loses its grip when the Word fills your heart. Meditation is not silent reading—it is focused reflection. It means turning a verse over in your heart until it shapes how you think, speak, and act. When the Word becomes your dominant thought, courage becomes your default response. Fill your spirit with faith-charged scriptures and let God's voice be louder than your fears.

2. Surround Yourself With Bold Believers

Proverbs 13:20 says, *"He that walketh with wise men shall be wise..."* and the same is true for faith. If you want to be bold, walk with the bold. Fear spreads through proximity, but so does courage. Surround yourself with people who talk victory, think big, pray with fire, and dream with heaven's blueprint. Avoid environments that tolerate small thinking, fear-based theology, or spiritual laziness. Iron sharpens iron. Your circle shapes your courage. Partner with those who remind you of who you are in Christ and challenge you to believe for more.

3. Declare God's Promises Over Your Life

Your mouth is not just for communication—it's a spiritual weapon. Proverbs 18:21 says, *"Death and life are in the power of the tongue..."* What you speak, you summon. Fearless faith is voiced faith. When you declare God's promises over your health, your finances, your mind, your marriage, your ministry, and your mission, you are activating heaven's power in those areas. Stop agreeing with fear and start agreeing with God. Replace, "I'm afraid this won't work," with "All things work together for my good." Your declarations either build strongholds or tear them down. Use your voice to build boldly.

4. Pray in the Spirit Consistently

Jude 1:20 says, *"But ye, beloved, building up yourselves on your most holy faith, praying in the Holy Ghost."* Praying in tongues is one of the most powerful tools for developing fearless faith. When you pray in the Spirit, you strengthen your inner man, align with the mind of Christ, and bypass your fears and doubts. Fear speaks the language of limitation, but tongues speak the language of heaven. A believer who prays in the Spirit regularly becomes spiritually alert, emotionally resilient, and mentally strong. If you want to grow in boldness, pray in tongues every day without apology.

5. Face Your Fears with the Truth of God's Word

Faith does not pretend that problems don't exist. It confronts fear with truth. John 8:32 says, *"And ye shall know the truth, and the truth shall make you free."* Every fear is rooted in a lie—but the Word of God is truth. When fear says, "You're not going to make it," the Word says, "I shall not die but live." When fear says, "You're alone," the Word says, "I will never leave you nor forsake you." Facing your fears doesn't mean you deny the challenge. It means you attack the lie behind it. And every time you do, fear loses power.

YOU ARE EQUIPPED FOR FEARLESS LIVING

You were not given a spirit of fear. It doesn't originate from God, so it has no right to remain. Instead, you have been endowed with power, love, and a sound mind, equipping you for a life without fear.

- **Power:** You possess divine strength to overcome challenges.

- **Love:** You are profoundly loved by God, and perfect love drives out fear (1 John 4:18).

- **A Sound Mind:** You can think clearly, make wise choices, and remain grounded.

Jesus approached storms, tombs, and hostile cities without fear. He resides within you, and His Spirit empowers you to do the same.

No matter the challenges you encounter, the Spirit within you is greater than any opposition. Allow faith to rise and fear to diminish. You are not a prisoner of fear; you are a warrior of faith.

FAITH DECLARATION

- I refuse to live in fear.

- I am bold, courageous, and filled with faith.

- God has not given me a spirit of fear.

- I possess power. I walk in love. My mind is clear and sound.

- No threat, delay, or obstacle can shake me.

- I trust in God, and I will not be swayed.

- I walk by faith, not by sight.

- I am fearless, and I am undefeated.

PRAYER POINTS:
FEARLESS FAITH

1. Father, thank You for granting me a spirit of power, love, and a sound mind.

2. I rebuke every spirit of fear and anxiety that seeks to undermine my faith.

3. Lord, expand my ability to believe in You boldly and obey without hesitation.

4. Let the fire of fearless faith rise within me like in the lives of Daniel, David, and Esther.

5. I declare that I will not succumb to fear; instead, I will stand in boldness and truth.

6. Father, empower me to proclaim faith even when facing storms and threats.

7. Every voice of doubt and discouragement, be silenced in Jesus' name.

8. Lord, prepare my hands for battle and my heart for unwavering faith.

9. I align my thoughts with Your promises and reject every fearful imagination.

10. I declare that I will fulfill my destiny fearlessly. I am more than a conqueror.

CHAPTER FOUR
SET THE LORD BEFORE YOU

"I have set the Lord always before me: because he is at my right hand, I shall not be moved."

— PSALM 16:8 (KJV)

In 2010, a 33-year-old Chilean miner named Mario Sepúlveda found himself trapped underground with his team, buried alive nearly half a mile beneath the surface. With no food, light, or escape, they faced an unimaginable predicament for 69 days. Yet, when he was interviewed after their miraculous rescue, Mario shared a powerful sentiment: *"There were not 33 of us. There were 34. God never left the mine."*

While many around him succumbed to panic, Mario took on the role of a leader, guiding his fellow miners in daily prayers, singing hymns, and focusing on the presence of God. Instead of fixating on the chaos surrounding them, he kept his eyes on the Deliverer.

What you choose to focus on can profoundly influence your ability to survive. When you keep the Lord at the forefront of your mind, you don't just endure challenges—you emerge from them stronger, steadier, and undefeated.

When your heart is focused on God, your life becomes unshakeable. The secret to living without fear lies not in positive thinking or sheer willpower, but in being deeply rooted in God's presence. Victory isn't just about fighting battles; it's about being aware. Those who remain conscious of God's closeness walk with uncommon boldness, favor, and stability.

David wrote Psalm 16 not during a time of peace, but when he was surrounded by enemies. Yet he confidently declared, "I shall not be moved." Why? Because he had set the Lord before him. His attention was not on the size of the threat but on the faithfulness of his God.

Setting the Lord before you means living with a constant awareness of His presence, His power, and

His promises. It involves making Him the center of your decisions, desires, and daily direction. When God is at the forefront, fear takes a back seat.

LIVING WITH DIVINE CONSCIOUSNESS

Many believers recognize God but do not actively keep Him before them. Acknowledging God means recognizing Him occasionally. Setting Him before you means prioritizing Him constantly. It means He becomes your reference point in every situation.

Joseph is a perfect example. In Genesis 39, even in a foreign land and under intense pressure, he said, *"How then can I do this great wickedness, and sin against God?"* His awareness of God's presence kept him anchored in integrity and strength. He lived with an audience of One.

Divine consciousness sharpens your spiritual perception. When you're aware of God's presence, you don't panic in the storm. You don't crumble under pressure. You don't conform to the culture. Instead, you move with holy confidence, knowing that the Lord is with you.

THE POWER OF GOD'S PRESENCE IN BATTLE

Scripture reveals that the presence of God is the most powerful asset in warfare. The Israelites carried the Ark of the Covenant into battle because it represented God's presence. Whenever the Ark went ahead of them, they experienced victory. When it was absent or dishonored, defeat followed.

Exodus 33:15 records Moses saying, *"If thy presence go not with me, carry us not up hence."* Moses understood that strategies, manpower, and resources were useless without God. What made Israel different from every other nation was not their numbers or weapons—it was the presence of the Almighty.

When you carry the presence of God, you carry victory. Obstacles become opportunities. Opposition becomes advancement. You walk through fire and come out without the smell of smoke because the fourth Man is with you (Daniel 3:25).

A BIBLICAL EXAMPLE: DAVID—THE GOD-SET MINDSET

David was a man of war, a king, a poet, and a worshiper. But more than anything else, he was a man who consistently set the Lord before him. In

Psalm 16:8, he wrote, *"I have set the Lord always before me: because he is at my right hand, I shall not be moved."* This was not just a poetic statement; it was a lifestyle.

From the fields where he watched over sheep to the battlefield where he faced Goliath, and even in the cave while fleeing from Saul, David carried an unshakable awareness of God's presence. He wasn't fearless because of his physical strength or military training; he was fearless because his eyes were fixed on the Lord.

When David stood before Goliath, he didn't size up the giant—he magnified his God. *"You come to me with a sword, with a spear, and with a shield,"* he said, *"but I come to you in the name of the Lord of hosts"* (1 Samuel 17:45). That name was not just a tagline—it was a revelation. David had set the Lord before him long before he faced that giant. His confidence in battle was rooted in his covenant awareness.

The secret behind David's victories wasn't just strategy—it was his sense of presence. He cultivated a relationship with God not only in public but also in the quiet moments of his private life. He played his harp in the fields, penned psalms under the stars, and sought the Lord's guidance before every major decision. The ark of the covenant, symbolizing

God's glory, meant so much to him that he made it a priority to bring it back to Jerusalem, dancing joyfully before it.

Even in moments of failure, David instinctively ran toward God rather than away from Him. After his sin with Bathsheba, he didn't offer excuses or shift the blame. Instead, he cried out, *"Cast me not away from thy presence; and take not thy Holy Spirit from me"* (Psalm 51:11). His greatest fear was not losing his throne, but losing the presence of God.

This captures the essence of setting the Lord before you: making God your highest pursuit, your deepest anchor, and your first response. When the Lord is before you, His presence becomes your foundation, His voice becomes your guide, and His strength becomes your shield. Like David, you will face adversaries and difficult seasons, but you will remain steadfast.

HOW TO SET THE LORD BEFORE YOU DAILY

1. Begin Each Day With Intentional Focus

Start your day immersed in the Word and in prayer. Acknowledge His presence. Invite His guidance. Declare, *"Today, the Lord is before me. I shall not be moved."*

2. Build Your Decisions Around His Will

When faced with choices—be it personal, financial, or ministry-related—ask yourself, *"What honors God in this?"* Keeping Him as your reference point helps you avoid mistakes.

3. Cultivate God-Awareness Throughout Your Day

You don't need a pulpit to be aware of God. In your car, at your desk, or while doing chores, stay connected. Whisper prayers, meditate on scripture, and thank Him for His closeness.

4. Let Worship be Your Atmosphere

Worship is more than just music; it's about surrender. When your heart is in constant worship, you're setting the Lord before you. He dwells in the praises of His people (Psalm 22:3).

5. Practice Stillness and Spiritual Sensitivity

Be still and know that He is God (Psalm 46:10). Quiet the noise around you and allow His Spirit to speak. The more attuned you are to Him, the more profoundly He'll work in you.

WHEN GOD IS BEFORE YOU, NOTHING CAN MOVE YOU

You remain steadfast when the Lord is your focus. The storms may rage, enemies may gather, and delays may occur. Yet, like David, you can confidently say, *"I shall not be moved."* Why? Because God is at your right hand. His presence secures your path, strengthens your heart, and fills you with courage.

In Psalm 23, David proclaimed, *"Though I walk through the valley of the shadow of death, I will fear no evil: for thou art with me."* For David, God's presence was not just a concept; it was his source of strength. He understood that the Shepherd was always near, even in the darkest times.

You don't need to feel God's presence to trust Him. His Word assures us that He will never leave you nor forsake you (Hebrews 13:5). Keep Him before you, and you will walk through fire, cross rivers, face giants, and emerge victorious.

FAITH DECLARATION

- I set the Lord always before me.

- I will not be moved.

- His presence goes with me, surrounds me, and strengthens me.

- I walk in divine focus and spiritual awareness.

- I will not fear what man or demons can do.

- I live anchored in the presence of God.

- I am undefeated because God is at my right hand.

PRAYER POINTS:
SETTING THE LORD BEFORE YOU

1. Father, thank You for being ever-present in my life. I acknowledge Your presence today.

2. Lord, help me to set You before me in all my ways, thoughts, and actions.

3. Let my heart remain sensitive to Your voice and guidance each day.

4. Remove every distraction that diverts my focus from You.

5. Surround me with Your presence and help me live with unshakable confidence.

6. I declare that because You are with me, I shall not be moved or shaken.

7. Teach me to prioritize Your presence above all else.

8. Let worship rise in my heart and transform the atmosphere around me.

9. I break every pattern of self-reliance and fully yield to Your leadership.

10. I decree that as I set You before me, I walk in peace, power, and victory.

CHAPTER FIVE

SPEAK LIFE, LIVE POWERFULLY

"Death and life are in the power of the tongue: and they that love it shall eat the fruit thereof."

— PROVERBS 18:21 (KJV)

Words have the remarkable ability to shape our reality. They carry a creative force, spiritual consequences, and lasting impacts across generations. When you speak, you're not just making noise—you're either planting seeds of life or sowing seeds of death. This isn't just motivational talk; it's a profound truth from the Kingdom. As Proverbs 18:21 reminds us, your mouth holds the power to activate either destruction or destiny.

One of the most significant revelations a believer can grasp is this: **You will never live above the level of your confession.** You can't experience victory while constantly speaking defeat. You can't thrive in life while recounting your failures. The words you speak either invite the assistance of angels or the interference of demons. The tongue may seem small, but it is the steering wheel of your future.

God spoke the universe into existence, setting a pattern from the very beginning. *"And God said... and it was so."* As children of God, created in His image, we are not just meant to talk—we are meant to rule through our words. Faith is voice-activated; dominion is voice-released. When you choose to speak life, you give heaven permission to act. When you choose to speak death, you align with negativity. Either way, the spiritual realm responds.

THE POWER OF YOUR VOICE

Your words have more significance than you may realize. In Numbers 14:28, God says, *"As you have spoken in my ears, so will I do."* That's a serious commitment. What you consistently express becomes your chosen reality. The Israelites wandered for 40 years not because God couldn't deliver the promised land, but because they continually spoke words of fear, inferiority, and defeat.

Jesus made this clear: *"For by your words you will be justified, and by your words you will be condemned"* (Matthew 12:37). Your words hold judicial power in the spiritual realm. They aren't trivial; they are covenantal. What you declare in times of challenge often matters more than what you pray in private.

Your future isn't solely determined in the heavenly courtroom. It is also shaped at the altar of your lips. If you want to transform your life, begin with your language.

LIVING THE SPEAK-LIFE LIFESTYLE

Let's explore the kind of speech that holds real power.

There was a moment when Jesus was walking with His disciples and noticed a fig tree filled with leaves but lacking fruit. Without a second thought, He declared: *"No man eat fruit of thee hereafter forever."* By the next day, that tree had withered from the roots (Mark 11:14, 20). Jesus didn't pray about it; He spoke to it. By doing so, He taught His disciples—and us—that whatever we say, believing, we shall receive.

Jesus spoke to storms, and they calmed. He addressed demons, and they fled. He commanded sickness, and it departed. He even spoke to the dead, and they came back to life. This wasn't just a demonstration of spirituality; it was an exhibition of divine authority through words. And we are called to operate in the same way.

In Ezekiel 37, God brought the prophet to a valley filled with dry bones—lifeless, hopeless, and scattered. God posed a question: *"Can these bones live?"* Instead of taking action Himself, God instructed Ezekiel, *"Prophesy unto these bones..."* As the prophet spoke, the bones came together. As he continued to speak, breath entered them, transforming them into a mighty army. What revived that valley? It wasn't emotion or activity; it was the **spoken Word** under divine instruction.

Similarly, David didn't wait for the outcome before he spoke. He declared before he released the stone: *"This day will the Lord deliver thee into my hand... I will smite thee, and take thine head..."* (1 Samuel 17:46). Notice how David set the outcome with his words. He declared victory before the battle. He didn't fight to win; he spoke the victory first, then engaged in the fight.

That's how you live undefeated. **You speak victory before you see it.** You declare healing when your body is in pain. You proclaim peace when storms rage. You assert provision when the account suggests otherwise. Your voice shapes your future.

THE ENEMY WANTS YOUR VOICE

Satan cannot stop God's plan for your life, so he targets your words. If he can get you to complain, voice doubt, confess fear, or dwell on defeat, he can stall your destiny. The enemy doesn't just present temptation; he initiates conversation.

In the Garden, Satan didn't wield a sword—he wielded words. *"Did God really say…?"* (Genesis 3:1). That's how the enemy operates. He plants seeds of doubt, waiting for you to nurture them with your speech. Once you begin to speak in agreement with him, you empower his lies.

You defeat Satan not by engaging in debate, but by declaring truth. When Jesus was tempted, He didn't enter into a conversation. He replied, *"It is written…"* three times (Matthew 4). That is how you speak life—by proclaiming the written Word with conviction. Don't combat thoughts with thoughts. Combat thoughts with words.

SPEAKING LIFE OVER EVERY AREA

1. Over Your Mind

Declare daily: *"I have the mind of Christ. I think with clarity and peace. I reject every lie and meditate on what is true."*

— *2 Timothy 1:7, Philippians 4:8, 1 Corinthians 2:16*

2. Over Your Health

Say boldly: *"By His stripes I am healed. Sickness cannot stay in my body. I walk in divine health."*

Isaiah 53:5, Psalm 103:2–3, 3 John 1:2

3. Over Your Finances

Confess: *"The Lord is my Shepherd, I shall not want. I walk in abundance, favor, and provision."*

— *Philippians 4:19, Psalm 23:1, Deuteronomy 8:18*

4. Over Your Family

Proclaim: *"My children are taught of the Lord. My home is blessed, peaceful, and protected."*

— *Isaiah 54:13, Psalm 112:2–3, Joshua 24:15*

5. Over Your Destiny

Affirm: *"I will fulfill purpose. Nothing will cut me short. God's hand is upon my life for good."*

— *Jeremiah 29:11, Psalm 138:8, Romans 8:28*

SILENCING NEGATIVE SPEECH HABITS

To speak life, you must first **uproot toxic speech patterns**. You cannot build a palace of power on a foundation of poisonous words. Many believers undermine their own prayers, delay their breakthroughs, and hinder the flow of divine favor through what they allow to escape their lips. Your speech can either be a bridge or a barrier to what God desires to release. Here are five destructive habits that must be broken if you want your words to carry Kingdom weight:

1. Complaining

Complaining often reflects a lack of spiritual awareness. It tends to magnify our problems while minimizing God's presence in our lives. When we complain, we shift our focus from God's faithfulness to the frustrations we experience. The children of Israel spent years wandering in the wilderness, not because of Pharaoh, but due to their own complaints. As God put it, *"How long shall I bear with this evil congregation, which murmur against me?"* (Numbers 14:27). He labeled their complaining as "evil." In contrast, gratitude embodies faith. It proclaims, "Even though I don't see it yet, God is still good, and I trust Him." If you want to change your atmosphere, stop the murmuring and start expressing thankfulness. Praise can achieve what protests never will.

2. Self-Pity

Self-pity can feel like a deep pit. The longer you

linger there, the harder it becomes to escape. It often masquerades as honesty, but in reality, it's just disbelief wrapped in emotion. Self-pity whispers, "No one understands me. I'm all alone. I can't take this anymore." However, heaven doesn't respond to pity; it responds to faith. Even Elijah, who called down fire from heaven, found himself under a tree in self-pity, wishing for death. God didn't engage with his complaints. Instead, He nourished him, gave him strength, and encouraged him to rise and keep moving forward (1 Kings 19). You are not helpless. You are not abandoned. You are supported by God. The Holy Spirit is your Advocate, your Helper, and your Strengthener. Rise above self-pity and begin to envision your comeback.

3. Negative labels

The way you speak about yourself shapes your identity. Stop using phrases like, *"I'm just unlucky… I'm always overlooked… I'm not that kind of person… Nothing good ever happens to me."* These aren't just casual comments; they are prophecies that influence how you view yourself and how others perceive you. Proverbs 6:2 warns us, *"Thou art snared with the words of thy mouth."* When you label yourself based on pain, failure, or fear, you hinder your own destiny. Remove those false labels and replace them with God's truth. You are not cursed; you are chosen.

You are not forgotten; you are favored. You are not limited; you are filled with purpose. Speak what God says about you, not what life has tried to define you as.

4. Fear-Based language

Fear-based language may appear wise and cautious, but it is rooted in doubt. It expresses thoughts like, *"What if I fail? What if the money doesn't come? What if I get sick? What if they reject me?"* These are seeds of fear that lead to delay and self-sabotage. Instead, change your perspective. Ask, *"What if God shows up? What if I succeed beyond my wildest dreams? What if this step of faith transforms everything?"* Faith is bold and forward-moving. It doesn't focus on failure; it anticipates God's intervention. Isaiah 41:10 reminds us, *"Fear thou not; for I am with thee."* If God is with you, then even the worst-case scenario holds no power. Let your words reflect trust, not fear. Speak as someone who knows heaven is on your side.

Jokes that Dishonor God's Promise

Words spoken in jest still carry significance in the spiritual realm. Just because you laughed when you said it doesn't mean the devil found it funny. Life and death are still present in humor. Mocking your own destiny, your calling, or your God-given *assignments*—

even in jest—opens the door to powerlessness. Sarcasm that undermines faith is still harmful. Jesus said, *"By your words you shall be justified…"* and that includes the words you didn't take seriously. There's nothing wrong with humor, but it should never come at the expense of truth. Let your speech be filled with grace, seasoned with salt (Colossians 4:6). You're not just a speaker; you're a sower. Sow wisely.

Your mouth should be an altar, not a trash bin. Let your words be intentional, not reckless. Speak what builds up. Declare what heals. Prophesy what aligns with heaven. Proverbs 13:3 states, *"He that keepeth his mouth keepeth his life: but he that openeth wide his lips shall have destruction."* In other words, using fewer careless words leads to fewer unnecessary battles. The more you discipline your tongue, the greater dominion you will experience.

YOU SHALL HAVE WHAT YOU SAY

Mark 11:23 contains one of the most radical promises in Scripture: *"Whosoever shall say… and shall not doubt… but shall believe that those things which he saith shall come to pass; he shall have whatsoever he saith."* The word **say** appears three times, while **believe** appears once.

Your declarations must be louder than your

observations. Faith doesn't speak what it sees; it speaks what it believes until it sees what it declares.

You will never rise above your confession. You must speak about where you are going, not where you've been. Your mountain needs your voice, not your silence. Declare boldly, even if your hands are trembling. Speak life, and you will live powerfully.

FAITH DECLARATION

- My mouth is a weapon of victory.

- I will speak life and not death.

- I agree with the Word of God.

- I cancel every negative word I've spoken over myself.

- I declare that I am blessed, favored, healed, and strong.

- No corrupt communication will come out of my mouth.

- My words build, heal, and create.

- I speak life, and I live powerfully—undefeated in Christ.

PRAYER POINTS:
SPEAK LIFE, LIVE POWERFULLY

1. Father, forgive me for every idle and negative word I have spoken.

2. Lord, anoint my mouth with fire. Let my tongue become an instrument of victory.

3. I break every self-imposed curse and release blessings over my life in Jesus' name.

4. Let every dry area in my life receive resurrection power through the Word of God.

5. I silence every lie of the enemy and replace it with divine truth.

6. Holy Spirit, train my mouth to speak in line with heaven.

7. I prophesy over my future: it is fruitful, glorious, and secured in Christ.

8. I reject the language of fear and embrace the language of faith.

9. My words shall no longer be casual—they shall carry authority.

10. As I speak life, let miracles break forth, and testimonies be born from my mouth.

CHAPTER SIX

THE WINNING MINDSET

❋

"And be not conformed to this world: but be ye transformed by the renewing of your mind..."
— ROMANS 12:2 (KJV)

In 1981, a woman named Terry Savage stood at the starting line of the Boston Marathon. What made her truly remarkable wasn't her speed—it was her mindset. Terry was blind. Running with a guide and tethered by a rope, she completed the entire 26.2 miles. When asked how she accomplished this feat, she said, *"I don't need to see the finish line—I just need to believe it's there and keep running toward it."*

That's the essence of a winning mindset. It perceives what others may overlook. It perseveres beyond obstacles that would hold most people back. It focuses on the promise ahead, rather than the problems in the way.

Victory begins in the mind long before it manifests in reality. And when your thoughts are shaped by God's truth, no limitation can keep you from moving forward.

Every battle is first won or lost in the mind. Before a giant falls, before a breakthrough manifests, before a healing appears, the heart must first believe and the mind must agree. You cannot live undefeated with a defeated mindset. If you are constantly thinking thoughts of fear, failure, or unworthiness, you will sabotage your own prayers with internal resistance. The transformation you seek begins with a transformation in your thinking.

God never intended for His children to live under mental oppression. He created you with the ability to think like Him, to see from heaven's perspective, and to live boldly in truth. However, the enemy is constantly at war in your thought life. His aim is to infect your imagination, distort your identity, and persuade you to settle for less than God's best. This is why Romans 12:2 urges us to be renewed in our minds. Though the battlefield may be spiritual, the mind is the control center.

You were not saved just to go to heaven; you were saved to reign in life. And reigning requires a renewed way of thinking. To live with a winning mindset means anchoring your thoughts in what God says, rather than what the world shouts. It involves rejecting small thoughts when God has called you to impact nations. It means refusing to dwell on pain when God has promised peace. Your mind must rise before your life can.

IDENTITY IS THE FOUNDATION OF VICTORY

You cannot walk in sustained victory without knowing who you are. When Jesus was baptized and the Father declared, *"This is my beloved Son, in whom I am well pleased,"* it was not for show. It was to reinforce His identity. Immediately after, Jesus was led into the wilderness, where the enemy attacked His identity with the words, *"If you are the Son of God…"* The first assault was not on His body but on His identity.

That same pattern continues today. The devil will do anything to make you forget who you are in Christ. If he can convince you that you are still a slave to sin, a powerless victim, or an unwanted outsider, he will neutralize your authority. But when you understand that you are a new creation, seated with Christ, filled with the Holy Spirit, and born to reign, you think and act differently.

Ephesians 2:6 states that you are seated with Christ in heavenly places. This means your perspective is above, not beneath. You don't live from earth toward heaven; you live from heaven toward earth. Your mindset is shaped by where you are seated, not by what you have endured. Winners think from victory, not for it.

THE MIND IS A GATEWAY, NOT A PRISON

God gave you the mind to process His thoughts and carry out His will on earth. However, many believers use their minds as prisons instead of gateways. They get stuck replaying past traumas, dwelling on what others have said, or worrying about worst-case scenarios. This is mental sabotage. 2 Corinthians 10:5 calls us to *"cast down imaginations, and every high thing that exalteth itself against the knowledge of God."* If it doesn't align with God's Word, it must be cast out.

Fear resides in an unrenewed mind. Doubt multiplies in thoughts that aren't filtered through truth. Your mind will either become a sanctuary for peace or a breeding ground for torment. You must choose daily to protect it. Philippians 4:8 is not just a suggestion—it's a strategy. Think on what is pure, lovely, of good report, and praiseworthy. Why? Because thoughts become words, and words shape your destiny.

A winning mindset speaks before the miracle. It declares before it sees. It doesn't wait for approval to believe. It stands on God's Word even when emotions suggest otherwise. This is how champions are made—not in easy times, but through disciplined thinking.

THE MIND OF CHRIST IS YOUR ADVANTAGE

1 Corinthians 2:16 says, *"But we have the mind of Christ."* This is not just a poetic idea; it is a reality for believers. If Jesus thought with clarity, confidence, and spiritual authority, so can you. He never panicked in storms. He never feared the Pharisees. He never second-guessed His Father. He walked in supernatural awareness and mental mastery.

You have access to that same mindset. But access alone is not enough; you must choose to think with it. This means filtering every decision, temptation, and challenge through a divine perspective. Ask yourself, *"What does the Word say about this? How would Jesus handle this?"* When your mind is submitted to truth, your life aligns with victory.

The enemy cannot dominate a mind anchored in Christ. He may attack, but he cannot win where Christ reigns. You don't need more opinions; you need a renewed mind. That is your advantage.

TRAUMA DOES NOT HAVE THE FINAL WORD

Many people find themselves feeling defeated mentally due to pain, loss, or betrayal. Trauma can be overwhelming, attempting to dictate your future based on your past experiences. However, the blood of Jesus not only offers forgiveness for sins but also transforms your identity. You don't have to carry the burdens of your trauma into the future. You are not beyond repair. You are not too far gone. You are not defined by what has happened to you.

Isaiah 26:3 promises, *"Thou wilt keep him in perfect peace, whose mind is stayed on thee: because he trusteth in thee."* God doesn't just heal our bodies; He also restores our minds. He reshapes our thought patterns. He frees us from obsessive thoughts, cycles of anxiety, and haunting memories. The power of the cross surpasses your past. Each day, affirm over your mind, "I have a sound mind. My thoughts are whole. I am not a prisoner to pain. I am free."

Your mindset can either limit you or elevate you. Choose to let it be the ladder that lifts you higher rather than the lid that holds you back.

TRAITS OF A WINNING MINDSET

A renewed, victorious mind consistently shows certain traits. These aren't merely attitudes; they are faith-driven practices that influence how champions think, live, and rise above challenges.

1. It Thinks Possibility, not limitation

A winning mind isn't confined by the question, "What if this doesn't work?" Instead, it dares to envision, "What if God does something even greater than I imagined?" Those who think in possibilities look beyond the present and see what can be achieved through faith. They don't dwell on problems; they embrace prophetic possibilities. While numbers may suggest failure, God says yes. Circumstances may urge patience, but faith declares it's time to act. With God, all things are possible, and the winning mind believes that wholeheartedly. It envisions the best, prepares for growth, and anticipates favor even in difficult times.

2. It Expects Victory, not Defeat

A winning mind starts each day with the expectation of breakthroughs, not setbacks. It proclaims, "This is the day the Lord has made. I will rejoice and succeed in it." Even before dawn breaks, it aligns itself with heaven's purpose. It doesn't brace for bad news or tread cautiously through the day, waiting for trouble. Instead, it stands confidently, knowing that victory is not a distant hope but a daily promise. This mindset doesn't question whether it will triumph; it understands that the outcome is already secured in Christ's victory.

3. It Refuses to Partner With Fear

Fear may knock, but a victorious mind never opens the door. It understands that fear is a liar, a thief of peace, and an enemy of progress. Instead of dwelling on "what if I fail," this mind responds with, "God is with me; I will not be afraid." Psalm 56:3 says, "What time I am afraid, I will trust in thee." The winning mindset consciously chooses not to entertain thoughts that elevate fear over faith. It treats fear like a virus that must be quarantined and eliminated with truth. The moment fear speaks, faith answers louder.

4. It Speaks Truth Even Under Pressure

When life puts pressure on the renewed mind, it doesn't spill out panic—it releases the Word. Pressure does not make it forget God's promises; instead, it makes those promises feel even more real. When lies try to surface and feelings contradict faith, this mind doesn't yield to emotion. It stands firm on the rock of Scripture and declares what God says. Like Jesus in the wilderness, the winning mind responds to every temptation and accusation with, "It is written." It doesn't negotiate with defeat; it confronts it with truth. This is the mind that governs the tongue purposefully and fills the atmosphere with life-giving words.

5. It Focuses Forward

The winning mind refuses to remain stuck in the pain of yesterday. It does not allow past mistakes, failures, or missed opportunities to hold it back. Instead, it declares, "God is not finished with me yet." It leans into what is next, not what was. Philippians 3:13–14 says, "Forgetting those things which are behind, and reaching forth unto those things which are before." This mindset takes that literally. It does not deny the past, but it refuses to be defined by it. Every day is a new canvas, and the renewed mind paints it with the colors of faith, purpose, and expectation.

It knows that God's mercies are new every morning, and forward is the only direction worth moving in.

FAITH DECLARATION

- My mind is renewed.

- I think God's thoughts.

- I pull down every stronghold and take every thought captive.

- I do not entertain fear, doubt, or defeat.

- I live with clarity, peace, and expectation.

- I have the mind of Christ.

- I think like a winner.

- I walk like a champion.

- I am undefeated in thought and victorious in life.

PRAYER POINTS:
THE WINNING MINDSET

1. Lord, I give my mind to You. Help my thoughts to be rooted in Your truth.

2. I reject any lies that tell me I am limited, broken, or unworthy.

3. Holy Spirit, please refresh my thinking each day with Your revelation and truth.

4. I dismantle every stronghold, toxic thought, and habit that stands in the way of my destiny.

5. May the mind of Christ be fully at work in me, guiding my decisions.

6. I embrace peace, clarity, and a sound mind through the blood of Jesus.

7. Every mental chain from my past is broken now. I am free to look forward.

8. Teach me to speak life-giving thoughts, even under pressure.

9. I walk in wisdom, discernment, and mental victory.

10. My thoughts are aligned with truth, and my life reflects victory. I am undefeated.

CHAPTER SEVEN

NEVER ALONE, ALWAYS BACKED

"The Lord of hosts is with us; the God of Jacob is our refuge."

— PSALM 46:7

You are never alone. Not for a second. Not in the darkest moment. Not in the fiercest battle. If you belong to Jesus Christ, you are never without support. Heaven does not abandon its own. You may feel outnumbered, but you are not outpowered. You may be surrounded by threats, but you are also surrounded by divine assistance. The child of God walks with covenant protection and Kingdom backing.

God never sends His people into a fight without

the assurance of His presence. Whether it's Daniel in the lions' den, Esther before the king, or the apostles standing before their persecutors, divine support is a consistent theme throughout scripture. The awareness of God's presence is what separates the fearful from the fearless. Those who know they are backed up speak differently, walk differently, and overcome differently.

Psalm 91 reminds us that a thousand may fall at your side, ten thousand at your right hand, but it will not come near you. Why? Because angels are assigned to keep you in all your ways. Because the Most High is your dwelling place. Because you are never alone. The believer who walks in victory is the one who lives with this awareness. He does not depend on feelings. He depends on the covenant.

GOD'S PRESENCE MAKES YOU DANGEROUS

When David said in Psalm 16:8, *"I have set the Lord always before me: because He is at my right hand, I shall not be moved,"* he was declaring more than poetic devotion. He was establishing a spiritual reality. The presence of God was not a vague idea to him; it was his weapon. David knew that Goliath was not just facing a young man with a slingshot, but a covenant man backed by the Lord of Hosts.

You too are a carrier of God's presence. If you are in Christ, the Spirit of God dwells in you. You are not just walking with God—you are walking in God. This awareness changes how you handle spiritual warfare. You stop begging for deliverance and start enforcing it. You stop panicking over attacks and start prophesying your victory. Demons do not tremble because of your volume; they tremble because of your backing.

God told Joshua, *"As I was with Moses, so I will be with you. I will not leave you nor forsake you"* (Joshua 1:5). That promise still holds true today. The same power that supported Moses in front of Pharaoh supports you in your own challenges. You are never alone—whether in courtrooms, hospital rooms, boardrooms, or during prayer. You are backed by heaven's authority and its army.

ANGELS ARE ON ASSIGNMENT

Psalm 34:7 states, *"The angel of the Lord encampeth round about them that fear him, and delivereth them."* You are not alone as you navigate through danger. Angels surround you, not as mere decorations, but as fierce warriors dedicated to your protection. They respond to God's commands and the declarations of believers.

Hebrews 1:14 tells us that angels are *"ministering spirits sent forth to minister for them who shall be heirs of salvation."* This means that angelic assistance is not just a bonus; it is part of your inheritance. When you declare God's Word, angels are sent out. When you pray in alignment with His will, angels are activated. When you take steps of faith, they join you on your journey.

This reality is illustrated in 2 Kings 6, where Elisha's servant was frightened by the enemy surrounding them. Elisha prayed, "Lord, open his eyes." Suddenly, the servant saw horses and chariots of fire surrounding Elisha. The enemy seemed numerous, but heaven's army was far greater. This is true for you as well. There are more on your side than against you. Your angels remain calm, and so should you.

THE HOLY SPIRIT IS YOUR ADVANTAGE

In addition to angelic help, God has given you an even greater gift—His Spirit. The Holy Spirit is not merely a power or a force; He is a person. He is your Helper, Comforter, Counselor, Advocate, Intercessor, and Strengthener. He is your divine advantage. Jesus said in John 14:16, *"I will pray the Father, and he shall give you another Comforter, that he may abide with you forever."* This means you will never experience a moment without Him.

The Holy Spirit guides you into truth, convicts you of righteousness, empowers you to pray, and reveals what lies ahead. He strengthens your inner self and makes your weaknesses irrelevant. He doesn't just walk beside you; He resides within you. This is the highest form of divine partnership. You're not stepping into your future with uncertainty; you're walking forward with wisdom from above.

Romans 8:26 tells us that the Spirit helps us in our weaknesses and even prays for us with groans that words cannot express. When you're unsure of what to say, He intercedes. When you don't know what decision to make, He guides you. When adversaries rise up, He raises a standard. You're not trying to be strong on your own; you are empowered from within.

THE POWER OF COVENANT BACKING

God is not just with you emotionally; He is with you legally. You are in covenant with the Almighty. A covenant is not a casual agreement; it is a binding promise sealed with blood. When Jesus shed His blood, He didn't just secure your salvation—He sealed your victory. This means all of Heaven's resources are available to fulfill your destiny.

Isaiah 54:17 states, *"No weapon that is formed against thee shall prosper; and every tongue that shall rise against thee in judgment thou shalt condemn."* Why? Because you are in covenant. God is obligated by His very nature to defend what belongs to Him. The blood of Jesus is your receipt, proof that you are backed, covered, and protected.

In 1 Samuel 17, David ran toward Goliath declaring, *"You come to me with a sword and a spear, but I come to you in the name of the Lord of Hosts."* That's covenant language. David understood that the battle was not just between him and Goliath; it was between Goliath and the God who supported David. That same God supports you.

YOU ARE A MOVING FORTRESS

You may not see angels, feel the Spirit, or hear the armies of Heaven, but you are still surrounded by divine protection. You are a moving fortress. Psalm 125:2 says, *"As the mountains are round about Jerusalem, so the Lord is round about his people from henceforth even forever."* God is not just checking in and out of your life; He is always present, always powerful, and always engaged.

This awareness transforms the way you approach life. It alleviates panic. It dispels loneliness. It clears doubt. You're not competing for attention; you already have heaven's focus on you. You're not waiting for help; assistance is already with you. Walk confidently, knowing you are supported. Pray as one who is covered. Speak boldly, without fear.

FAITH DECLARATION

- I am never alone.

- God is with me.

- Angels are assigned to me.

- The Holy Spirit dwells within me.

- I walk in divine protection and receive supernatural guidance.

- I do not panic; I am covered by covenant.

- I have support in every battle and reinforcement in every storm.

- I am never abandoned; I am always backed.

- I walk with confidence because I am undefeated.

PRAYER POINTS:
NEVER ALONE, ALWAYS BACKED

1. Father, thank You for always being with me. I embrace a renewed awareness of Your presence.

2. I declare that I am protected by the blood and safeguarded by Your covenant.

3. Holy Spirit, guide me into truth and grant me discernment in all my decisions.

4. I release angelic assistance over my family, my journey, and my responsibilities.

5. May every fear of abandonment be shattered by the reality of Your closeness.

6. I stand boldly, knowing I am surrounded by heaven's army.

7. Lord, help me to always recognize the power that supports me.

8. I command every opposing force to bow before the God who protects me.

9. Teach me to walk with covenant confidence each day.

10. I will not be shaken. I am surrounded. I am undefeated.

CHAPTER EIGHT

VICTORY IN SPIRITUAL WARFARE

⸺◈⸺

"For the weapons of our warfare are not carnal, but mighty through God to the pulling down of strong holds."

— 2 CORINTHIANS 10:4

During World War II, the Allied forces devised a clever strategy known as "Operation Bodyguard." This involved creating fake armies, sending out phantom radio signals, and spreading false intelligence to mislead the enemy. Remarkably, it worked. The Nazis were tricked into moving their forces in the wrong direction, which ultimately paved the way for the D-Day invasion that would change the course of the war.

In a similar way, Satan operates through deception, intimidation, and spiritual misdirection. However, when a believer walks in discernment, truth, and divine authority, every trap is revealed, and every lie crumbles.

Spiritual warfare isn't just about battling demons— it's about refusing to be fooled by the enemy's illusions. The victory is already yours, but you need to stand firm, equipped, and vigilant.

The Christian life is not a playground; it is a battleground. But the good news is—we win. We are not fighting for victory; we are fighting from victory. Jesus has already conquered the enemy. Our role is to enforce the victory He secured with His blood. The moment you were born again, you were enlisted in a war. But don't worry; you were also equipped.

Spiritual warfare is real. Whether you feel it or not, you are in the midst of an invisible battle. But this battle isn't fought with fists or physical weapons; it's fought with truth, prayer, faith, and the authority of the Word. The devil isn't after your personality; he's after your position. He knows that if you ever realize the authority you carry, his schemes will crumble beneath you.

This is not the time for a passive approach to your faith. You cannot win spiritual battles with a casual attitude. If you don't recognize that you're in a fight, you will live like a victim instead of a victor. But once you rise in understanding and begin to operate in your God-given authority, you become a threat to the kingdom of darkness. You become *undefeated*.

THE NATURE OF THE WARFARE

Paul makes it clear in Ephesians 6:12— *"For we wrestle not against flesh and blood, but against principalities, against powers, against the rulers of the darkness of this world..."* This fight is not against people; it is against demonic structures and invisible forces that work to resist God's plan in your life.

The enemy uses deception, distraction, and intimidation. He whispers lies, fuels discouragement, and sets traps through fear, temptation, and shame. However, he has no real power over a believer who knows their authority. He is a defeated foe pretending to be a threat. Jesus said in Luke 10:19, *"Behold, I give unto you power… over all the power of the enemy: and nothing shall by any means hurt you."*

Victory begins with recognition. When you realize that your struggle is spiritual, you stop reacting emotionally. You stop fighting people and start confronting the spirit behind the storm. Spiritual maturity requires spiritual discernment. Not every delay is natural, and not every conflict is random. Some issues must be addressed in prayer rather than in arguments.

YOUR SPIRITUAL ARSENAL

You are not left defenseless in this battle. God has not called you to war without equipping you with weapons that are guaranteed to win. You don't need to fear what's against you when you're fully aware of what's working for you. Heaven has provided a supernatural arsenal for you to walk in daily victory—if you know it, believe it, and use it.

1. The Name of Jesus

The Name of Jesus isn't just a religious phrase—it's a powerful spiritual weapon. Philippians 2:10 tells us that at the name of Jesus, *"every knee should bow, of things in heaven, and things in earth, and things under the earth."* This includes demons, illnesses, curses, and every force of darkness. The Name of Jesus is your badge of divine authority. When you speak it with faith, hell takes notice. That Name grants you the right to command, resist, bind, and release in the spiritual realm. You're not acting on your own strength—you're coming in His Name. Everything must bow to it.

2. The Word of God

The Word isn't just for study—it's your sword. Ephesians 6:17 reminds us to *"Take... the sword of the Spirit, which is the word of God."* Jesus showed us how to wield this sword when He faced Satan in the wilderness. He didn't argue or plead; He simply declared, *"It is written."* That's your strategy. When fear arises, declare the Word. When temptation approaches, speak the truth. When you're under pressure, unleash scripture. This isn't about memorization; it's about spiritual enforcement. The Word in your mouth carries the same power as the Word in God's mouth. It never fails.

3. The Blood of Jesus

There's no weapon in hell that can overcome the power of the blood. Revelation 12:11 states, *"They overcame him by the blood of the Lamb..."* The blood is your receipt, proving that the price for your victory has already been paid. It speaks of mercy, deliverance, healing, restoration, and triumph; better things than the blood of Abel. The blood is your covering. Apply it over your home, your family, your future, and your finances. When the enemy sees the blood, he must pass over. In places where the blood is honored, demonic activity is silenced. Use it boldly. Declare it daily. Plead it fervently. The blood still works.

4. The Armor of God

Spiritual warfare calls for spiritual protection, which is why God has equipped you with the full armor. Ephesians 6:13–18 details this armor: the helmet of salvation protects your thoughts; the breastplate of righteousness safeguards your heart; the belt of truth secures your identity; the shield of faith extinguishes fiery darts; the sword of the Spirit combats deception; and the shoes of peace keep you steady. This armor isn't just a recommendation; it's essential for survival. Wear it through prayer, meditation, and declaration. Speak it aloud. Visualize it. Live it. You don't just don the armor, you embody it.

5. The Power of Praise

Praise is more than just sound; it's a powerful weapon that can open prison doors and break chains. In Acts 16:25–26, we see Paul and Silas in prison, shrouded in darkness, yet they chose to sing praises. Heaven responded with an earthquake. That's the power of praise—it transforms environments, activates angels, silences oppression, and invites divine help. When the enemy tries to bring you down, praise your way to freedom. When life feels chaotic, choose praise over complaints. Praise confuses the adversary and magnifies your God. It turns your battleground into a place of breakthroughs. Praise is your battle cry for victory.

6. Praying in the Spirit

You can't afford to fight the battle using just your understanding. Romans 8:26 tells us that the Holy Spirit assists us in prayer when we're unsure of what to say. When you pray in the Spirit, especially in tongues, you connect directly with God's mind, surpassing your intellect and aligning with heavenly strategies. Speaking in tongues strengthens your spirit, disarms demonic forces, and reveals hidden truths. It's your direct line to the throne room. This practice is essential, not optional. The early church frequently prayed in the Spirit and witnessed incredible power. You should do the same. Praying in tongues sharpens your discernment, ignites your courage, and keeps you spiritually resilient in a world filled with challenges.

TERRITORY MUST BE TAKEN, NOT JUST DEFENDED

Many believers focus solely on defense. They pray only when under attack and speak the Word only after experiencing loss. But those who remain undefeated take the initiative. They claim territory and declare peace before the storms arise. They embrace promises before the battles begin.

Jesus said in Matthew 11:12, *"The kingdom of heaven suffereth violence, and the violent take it by force."* This doesn't refer to physical aggression but to spiritual intensity. You can't achieve victory with casual prayers. You must be fervent in your faith, bold in your declarations, consistent in your efforts, and relentless in your stand.

There are specific areas meant for you: spiritually, financially, geographically, and generationally. The enemy has no claim to them. However, until you rise up and fight for what is rightfully yours, you may find yourself stuck in the same place. Enough is enough. This is your season to reclaim everything that belongs to you.

MAINTAINING VICTORY THROUGH RESISTANCE

James 4:7 reveals the key to ongoing victory— *"Submit yourselves therefore to God. Resist the devil, and he will flee from you."* Submission acts as your shield, while resistance serves as your sword. When your life aligns with God, your authority becomes unshakeable. The enemy cannot accuse you where there is submission, nor can he stay where there is resistance.

Victory isn't just a one-time achievement; it's a lifestyle of refusing to give up. It's about waking up each day as a soldier, standing firm in the spiritual realm. It involves safeguarding your peace, protecting your boundaries, and watching over your family. It's about choosing to walk in the light, even when darkness tries to lure you in. You don't just want victory in moments—you desire dominion as a way of life.

FAITH DECLARATION

- I am armed and ready.

- I am not fighting for victory—I fight from a place of victory.

- The weapons of my warfare are powerful through God.

- I cover my life with the blood of Jesus.

- I resist the enemy, and he flees from me.

- I am not afraid. I am vigilant. I am equipped.

- My territory is secure. My future is safeguarded.

- I walk in daily victory in Jesus' name.

PRAYER POINTS:
VICTORY IN SPIRITUAL WARFARE

1. Lord, awaken my spiritual senses to recognize every battle around me.

2. I declare that I am not a victim; I am a victor through Christ.

3. I put on the whole armor of God. I am covered and equipped.

4. Every assignment of the enemy against me, be dismantled in Jesus' name.

5. Let the blood of Jesus speak over my family, my mind, and my destiny.

6. I bring clarity and confidence to my side, knowing that no weapon formed against me will succeed

7. I embrace peace, healing, and restoration in the midst of every storm I face.

8. I reject every lie, fear, and accusation, replacing them with the truth of God's Word.

9. Father, guide my actions and strengthen my resolve in every battle I encounter.

10. Thank You, Lord, for the continuous victory I experience in my life. I stand strong and undefeated in Christ.

CHAPTER NINE

UNDEFEATED AND
UNSTOPPABLE

*"What shall we then say to these things? If
God be for us, who can be against us?"*

— ROMANS 8:31

In 1992, British sprinter Derek Redmond entered the
Olympic Games as a favorite to win the 400-meter
race. However, halfway through the semifinal,
he tore his hamstring and collapsed on the track.
Overcome with pain and tears, he got back up and
began limping toward the finish line. Then, from
the stands, his father broke through security, ran to
his son, and supported him as they made their way
together to the end.

The stadium erupted in applause. Derek didn't win the race, but he finished it—with help.

That moment embodies what it means to live an undefeated life. It's not about avoiding pain, but about refusing to give up. It's about leaning on the Father and crossing the finish line, even when you're hurting.

You might be limping, but if God is by your side, you are still moving forward. And as long as you're moving, you're still winning.

Living an undefeated life goes beyond merely surviving; it's about making progress. It's not just about getting through challenges, but about rising, reigning, and representing the Kingdom with authority. You were not saved to remain stagnant; you were saved to be unstoppable.

When Jesus declared, *"I will build My church, and the gates of hell shall not prevail against it,"* He wasn't talking about a timid, passive group of believers. He envisioned a bold, fearless community that advances despite opposition. That includes you. The church operates on offense, not defense. You're not just holding your ground; you're claiming new territory.

God didn't bring you this far to abandon you. He

didn't redeem you through sacrifice just for you to be crushed by pressure. The God who began a good work in you is dedicated to seeing it through to completion. Your future is already marked by victory. The enemy can only attempt to intimidate you into giving up. But if you choose not to quit, you become unstoppable.

THE POWER OF PERSEVERANCE

Unstoppable believers aren't always the most talented or the most connected. They are simply those who refuse to back down. They are driven by the conviction that what God says is final. They are undeterred by delays, detours, or discouragement. They outlast storms. They outpray opposition. They outfaith resistance.

Hebrews 10:35–36 reminds us, *"Cast not away therefore your confidence, which hath great recompence of reward. For ye have need of patience, that, after ye have done the will of God, ye might receive the promise."* This means the promise is not in question—your endurance is. The enemy is not attacking your present; he's trying to weaken your perseverance.

Being unstoppable doesn't mean facing no opposition; it means being unshakable in the face of it. The three Hebrew boys were thrown into the fire, but the flames could not consume them. Daniel was cast into the lions' den, but the lions could not harm him. Paul faced beatings, stoning, and shipwrecks, yet he completed his journey. You too must embrace the mindset that says, "No matter what happens, I will not break."

HOW TO DEVELOP A PERSEVERING SPIRIT

Developing spiritual perseverance is not automatic—it must be cultivated intentionally. Here's how to build staying power that makes you truly UNDEFEATED:

- **Stay Anchored in the Word**

  The Word of God is your foundation. When storms come, you don't stand on feelings—you stand on truth. Feed your spirit daily with scriptures about endurance, strength, and victory. (Matthew 7:24–25, Psalm 1:2–3)

- **Practice Daily Obedience**

  Perseverance grows when you obey even when it's hard. Do what God told you, even when the excitement fades. Obedience fuels consistency, and consistency builds strength. (James 1:25)

- **Guard Your Confession**

  Don't cancel your faith with your words. Declare God's promises, even when circumstances contradict them. What you say in the delay determines whether you reach the promise. (Hebrews 10:23)

- **Surround Yourself with Faithful People**

  Walk with those who finish what they start. Encouragement and accountability from like-minded believers will keep you moving when you feel like quitting. (Hebrews 10:24–25)

- **Strengthen Yourself in the Lord**

  Like David in 1 Samuel 30:6, you must learn how to encourage yourself. Don't wait for others to cheer you on. Praise, pray, and stir your own spirit. Worship is your weapon.

- **Pray Through, Not Just About**

  Push in prayer until the burden lifts. Don't just talk about what you're going through—war through it. Prayer builds endurance like spiritual weight training. (Luke 18:1)

- **Focus Forward, Not Backward**

  Keep your eyes on where God is taking you, not what you've lost. Perseverance requires forward focus. Paul said, *"Forgetting what is behind and reaching toward what is ahead..."* (Philippians 3:13–14)

- **Remember Past Victories**

  Rehearse what God has already brought you through. If He did it before, He'll do it again. Past victories build present confidence. (Psalm 77:11)

- **Lean on the Holy Spirit**

  You don't have to endure in your own strength. The Spirit empowers you to keep going. Ask for fresh grace daily to walk, run, and keep standing. (Isaiah 40:31)

- **Refuse to Quit. Period!**

  Make a quality decision: "No matter what, I'm not giving up." The devil's greatest weapon is discouragement. Your greatest counterattack is determination. The reward is reserved for the one who endures to the end. (Matthew 24:13)

UNSTOPPABLE FAITH
SPEAKS BEFORE IT SEES

Faith is not silent. It speaks. Faith proclaims the end from the beginning. As Jesus said in Mark 11:23, *"Whosoever shall say unto this mountain… and shall not doubt in his heart… he shall have whatsoever he saith."* This is not just motivational talk; it's Kingdom truth. Mountains don't move by mere observation; they shift because you command them.

Your words shape your battles. When you speak in alignment with heaven, you pave the way for miracles. The enemy seeks to silence you with fear, doubt, or despair, believing he can halt your progress. But if you persist in speaking truth, declaring breakthroughs, and aligning your language with God's promises, your advancement becomes inevitable.

David proclaimed, *"I will not die, but live, and declare the works of the Lord."* That is unstoppable faith—speaking life amid death, proclaiming victory in the valley. It doesn't wait for conditions to improve to rejoice; it rejoices because it knows the outcome is already secured.

WALKING IN SUPERNATURAL MOMENTUM

When heaven supports you, there's a grace that accelerates your journey. What might have taken ten years can unfold in one. Delays transform into divine setups. Closed doors swing open effortlessly. This is walking in supernatural momentum. You aren't inching toward your destiny; you are propelled by favor.

Isaiah 60:22 states, *"I the Lord will hasten it in his time."* This means what once resisted you will now respond to you. What was stuck will start to move, and what was lost will be restored. With God's hand on your life, you will progress faster, higher, and farther than your qualifications suggest. Others may look at your achievements and wonder how it happened, but you will know—this is the Lord's doing.

To be unstoppable is to live in divine rhythm. It involves listening to the Holy Spirit, acting promptly, and avoiding distractions. The enemy excels at creating diversions. If he can't destroy you, he'll try to lead you off course. But when you follow the Spirit, you step into prepared places, divine encounters, and open heavens.

DESTINY CANNOT BE DENIED

You have a purpose that hell cannot thwart. You carry a prophetic future that no adversary can erase. You were not born by accident; you were appointed. Before your birth, God recorded your days in His book. The enemy may have attempted to derail you with childhood trauma, rejection, or failure, but it's too late. You are already destined for victory.

Romans 8:30 reassures us, *"Whom He predestinated, them He also called: and whom He called, them He also justified: and whom He justified, them He also glorified."* Your destiny is not a matter of choice; it's authored and supported by God. The only one who can hinder it is you—and you won't. Not after all God has invested in you. Not after all you have overcome.

This is not the time to shrink back. This is the time to surge forward. Let every gift awaken. Let every seed of purpose flourish. Let every delay become a platform. Let every "no" prepare you for a better "yes." You were created for this moment. You were made for this hour. You are undefeated and unstoppable.

FAITH DECLARATION

- I am a child of God.

- I am not fragile; I am fortified.

- I do not quit, back down, or shrink away.

- I speak with authority and move with boldness.

- Every delay is turning into divine acceleration.

- I walk in supernatural momentum.

- My destiny will not be denied.

- I am moving forward by grace and with power.

- I am undefeated and unstoppable.

PRAYER POINTS: UNDEFEATED AND UNSTOPPABLE

1. Lord, I thank You for destined me for victory and not defeat.

2. I declare that no weapon formed against me shall prosper. I move forward in faith.

3. Every mountain of resistance, be moved now in Jesus' name.

4. Father, accelerate my steps by Your hand. Let what was delayed be delivered.

5. I silence every voice of fear, failure, and discouragement. I rise in boldness.

6. Holy Spirit, guide me in divine rhythm and supernatural momentum.

7. I will finish my race. I will complete my assignment. I will fulfill my calling.

8. Let every hidden gift and purpose within me be awakened now.

9. I declare that nothing shall by any means stop me. I am carried by covenant.

10. I step into my next level with faith, fire, and focus. I am undefeated and unstoppable.

LIVING UNDEFEATED EVERY DAY

The journey of the undefeated believer is not a destination; it's a daily decision. It's about choosing to trust God when circumstances scream otherwise. It's about rising in faith when fear tries to paralyze you. It's about standing firm on the Word when the world shakes beneath you.

You are not weak. You are not forgotten. You are not abandoned. You are chosen, called, equipped, and supported by heaven's armies. You were born to win, born to lead, and born to rise. And with Christ in you, the hope of glory, you are destined to finish strong.

Let this be your declaration:

I was born for more. I will not quit, break, or bow. I am rising, claiming territory, speaking life, and advancing. I am undefeated because the Greater One lives in me.

So, move forward. Fight the good fight of faith. Speak the Word. Enforce your victory. And never forget, no matter the battle, no matter the storm, you are not alone. You are never without backup. You are UNDEFEATED!

www.ingramcontent.com/pod-product-compliance
Lightning Source LLC
Chambersburg PA
CBHW061657120626
46550CB00003B/971

"Reading Kristi's story felt like a privilege—her words are humble, loving, and deeply thoughtful. She champions a unique cancer journey that is both empowering and hopeful, offering wisdom for anyone seeking their own path to healing. A beautiful guide for those curious about natural healing and the courage it takes to find answers."

—Monica Pelle, RD, CPT,
Speaker, Coach, And Consultant

"This is a wonderful story of Kristi's journey to health, utilizing alternative treatments to fight cancer. It is a story of hard work, spirituality, and perseverance. It should be an inspiration to anyone fighting a cancer diagnosis. I was proud to be a part of Kristi's journey and health solution."

—John A. Rothchild, DDS

"In the same way we are taught to make use of Chinese medicine, it is very affirming that we must always strive to find the root of the illness. This story clearly came from the heart, honoring the people and places that so strongly contributed to her healing path. It was told without presumption and with the intention to help others who may also feel there is something missing in their attempt to find optimal health."

—Molly Gibson,
Licensed Acupuncturist and Chinese Medicine Practitioner

"We have witnessed Kristi's unwavering faith in God in every aspect of her life. That deep faith guided her through her battle with cancer. While everyone's journey is different and individual, I trust you will find her story to be uplifting and inspiring. I believe you will see how turning over all of our weaknesses and worries to our loving and life-sustaining Lord and Savior Jesus Christ will provide the peace and healing that only he can give."

—Dr. Thomas H. Stuebe, DC, and Dr. Donna A. Martos, DC,
New Life Chiropractic Center